Origami
Monsters

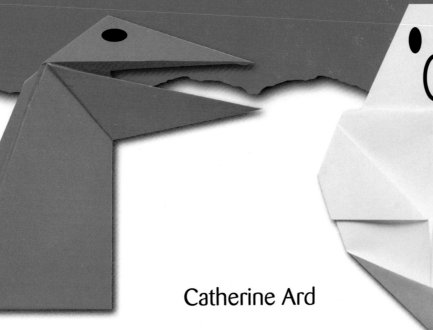

Catherine Ard

Gareth Stevens
PUBLISHING

Please visit our website, www.garethstevens.com. For a free color catalog of all our high-quality books, call toll free 1-800-542-2595 or fax 1-877-542-2596.

Library of Congress Cataloging-in-Publication Data

Ard, Catherine.
Origami monsters / by Catherine Ard.
p. cm. — (Amazing origami)
Includes index.
ISBN 978-1-4824-2262-7 (pbk.)
ISBN 978-1-4824-2263-4 (6-pack)
ISBN 978-1-4824-2201-6 (library binding)
1. Origami — Juvenile literature. 2. Monsters — Juvenile literature. I. Title.
TT870.A73 2015
736.982—d23

First Edition

Published in 2015 by
Gareth Stevens Publishing
111 East 14th Street, Suite 349
New York, NY 10003

Copyright © 2015 Arcturus Publishing

Models and photography: Michael Wiles
Text: Catherine Ard
Design: Emma Randall and Belinda Webster
Editor: Joe Harris
Monster photography: Shutterstock

Printed in the United States of America
CPSIA compliance information: Batch CW15GS: For further information contact
Gareth Stevens, New York, New York at 1-800-542-2595.

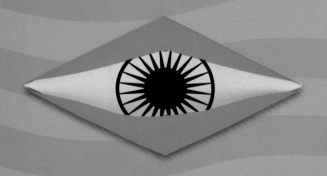

Contents

Basic folds

Origami has been popular in Japan for hundreds of years and is now loved all around the world. You can make great models with just one sheet of paper... and this book shows you how!

The paper used in origami is thin but strong, so that it can be folded many times. It is usually colored on one side. Alternatively, you can use ordinary scrap paper, but make sure it's not too thick.

Origami models often share the same folds and basic designs. This introduction explains some of the folds that you will need for the projects in this book. When making the models, follow the key below to find out what the lines and arrows mean. And always crease well!

KEY

valley fold `-------------` step fold (mountain and valley fold next to each other) direction to move paper ↘

mountain fold `..............` push ▼

MOUNTAIN FOLD

To make a mountain fold, fold the paper so that the crease is pointing up towards you, like a mountain.

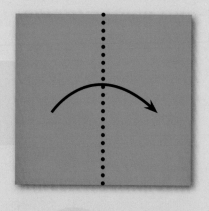
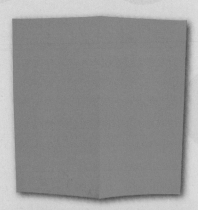

VALLEY FOLD

To make a valley fold, fold the paper the other way, so that the crease is pointing away from you, like a valley.

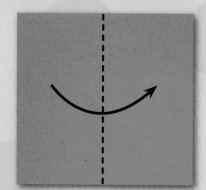

INSIDE REVERSE FOLD

An inside reverse fold is useful if you want to make a nose or a tail, or if you want to flatten off the shape of another part of an origami model.

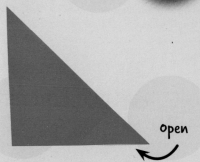

(1) Practice by first folding a piece of paper diagonally in half. Make a valley fold on one point and crease.

(2) It's important to make sure that the paper is creased well. Run your finger over the crease two or three times.

(3) Unfold and open up the corner slightly. Refold the crease nearest to you into a mountain fold.

Open

(4) Open up the paper a little more and then tuck the tip of the point inside. Close the paper. This is the view from the underside of the paper.

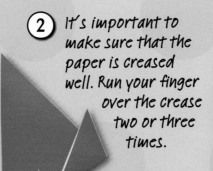

(5) Flatten the paper. You now have an inside reverse fold.

OUTSIDE REVERSE FOLD

An outside reverse fold is useful if you want to make a head, beak, or foot, or another part of your model that sticks out.

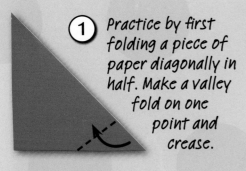

(1) Practice by first folding a piece of paper diagonally in half. Make a valley fold on one point and crease.

(2) It's important to make sure that the paper is creased well. Run your finger over the crease two or three times.

(3) Unfold and open up the corner slightly. Refold the crease farthest away from you into a valley fold.

Open

(4) Open up the paper a little more and start to turn the corner inside out. Then close the paper when the fold begins to turn.

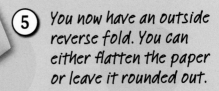

(5) You now have an outside reverse fold. You can either flatten the paper or leave it rounded out.

Frankenstein

Down in his secret laboratory, a mad scientist flicks a switch and his creepy creation shudders into life. Fold this fearsome Frankenstein face – if you dare!

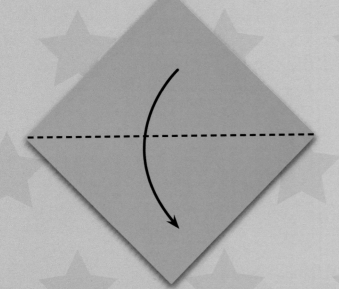

① Start with the paper colored side up and one point towards you. Valley fold in half from top to bottom, then unfold.

② Valley fold the top corner so that the point meets the center crease.

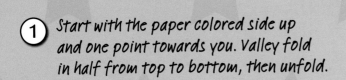

③ Make a crease about ¹/₂ inch (15 mm) from the top and fold the point up again.

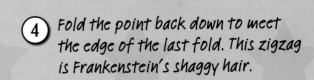

④ Fold the point back down to meet the edge of the last fold. This zigzag is Frankenstein's shaggy hair.

5 Make a step fold, starting with a valley fold just below the center. This is the monster's forehead.

6 To shape the face, mountain fold the right side from the edge of the zigzag.

Did You Know?

In the original story by Mary Shelley, Frankenstein is the name of the monster's creator. The monster doesn't have a name.

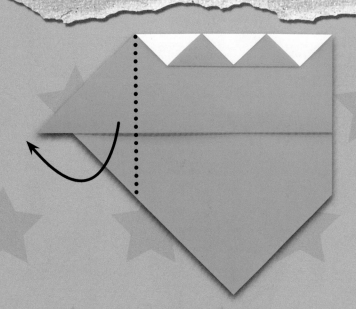

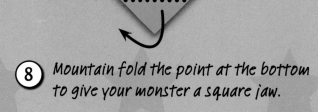

⑦ Mountain fold the left side in the same way.

⑧ Mountain fold the point at the bottom to give your monster a square jaw.

⑨ Draw a sad mouth, eyes and a scary scar to bring your monster to life. Why not fold a frightful girlfriend to keep your Frankenstein company?

Ghost

You don't need to hunt in haunted houses or creep around in graveyards in the dead of night. Fold this spooky model to see a paper ghost appear!

Use plain white origami paper, or pick a pale shade and start with the colored side facing up.

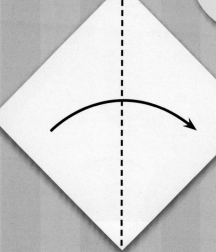

① Place the paper with one point towards you. Valley fold in half from left to right and unfold.

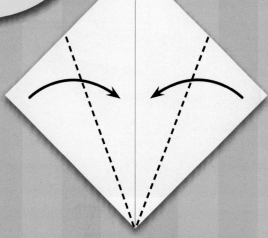

② Fold in the sides from the bottom corner so that the edges meet in the center. This makes a kite shape.

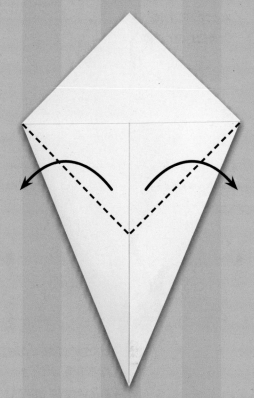

③ Valley fold the flaps on either side. The bottom edges should sit horizontally.

④ Turn the paper over.

Did You Know?

Ghosts are thought of as floating white figures, but there are also stories of ghost trains, phantom ships, and even ghostly animals!

5 Fold in the outer edges as shown.

6 Valley fold the sides from the top point to meet on the center crease.

7 Valley fold the top point down.

8 Make a step fold, starting with a valley fold across the center crease.

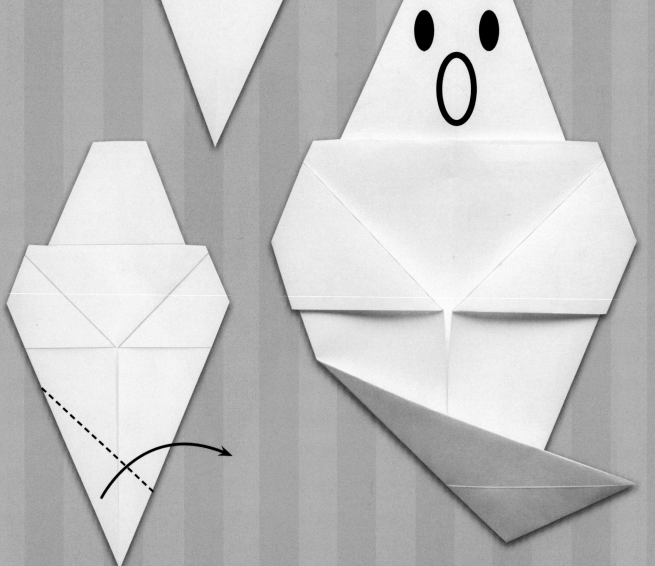

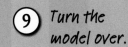

9 Turn the model over.

10 Make the ghost's wispy tail with a diagonal valley fold across the bottom point.

11 Draw the eyes and a wailing mouth. Your origami ghost is ready for some phantom fun! Woooooo!

The Gobbler

Look out! The ghastly gobbler is on the prowl for a tasty snack! Follow the steps to fold your own munching menace, then move his giant jaws to make him gobble, guzzle, and gulp!

Medium

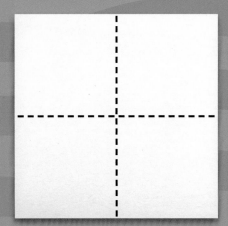

1) With the paper colored side down, fold from top to bottom and unfold, then from left to right and unfold.

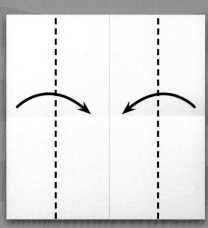

2) Valley fold the sides to meet the center crease.

3) Now valley fold the top and bottom edges to meet in the center.

4) You should have a square. Unfold the top and bottom.

5) Valley fold the corners to meet the first crease in.

6) Unfold the corners again.

OPEN

7) Open up the top left corner.

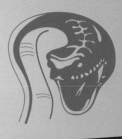

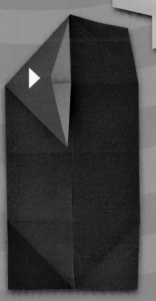

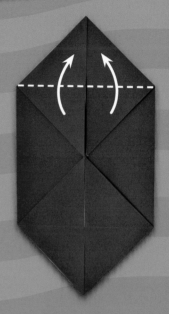

8 Pull the inner point down to the center crease and press the paper flat to make a triangle.

9 Repeat steps 7 and 8 on the other three corners.

10 Valley fold the flaps at the top.

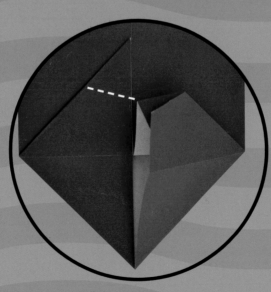

11 Valley fold the points on the bottom flaps, then unfold.

12 Tuck the points in with inside reverse folds.

13 Mountain fold the top half of the paper behind the bottom half.

14 Now mountain fold the top behind the point at the bottom.

15 You now have three triangular layers at the bottom. Fold up the top two. These are the lips.

16 Mountain fold the corners so that they line up with the bottom points.

SIDE VIEW

eyes

folded corners

top lip

bottom lip

17 Hold the model by the folded corners and open up the lips. Push in the sides to move the mouth.

18 Draw two eyes at the top. Now your gobbler is ready to guzzle his first meal – but who is on the menu?

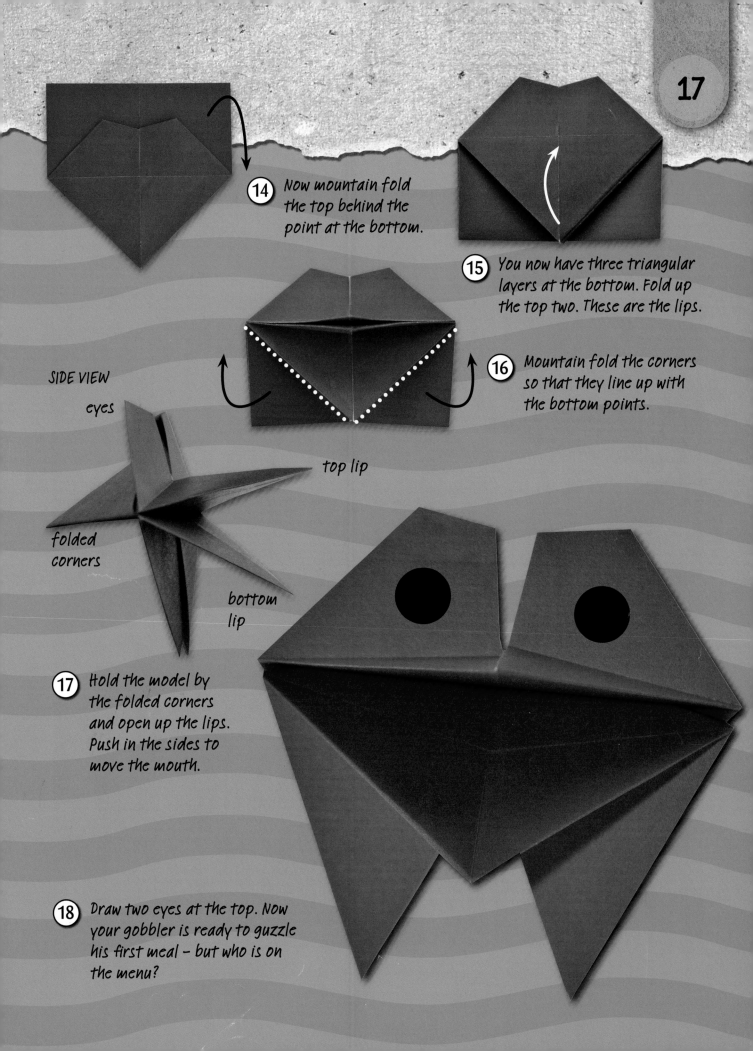

Cyclops Eye

Ever get the feeling you're being watched? There's no escaping the gaze of this goggling orb. Follow these steps to create a scary cyclops in the blink of an eye!

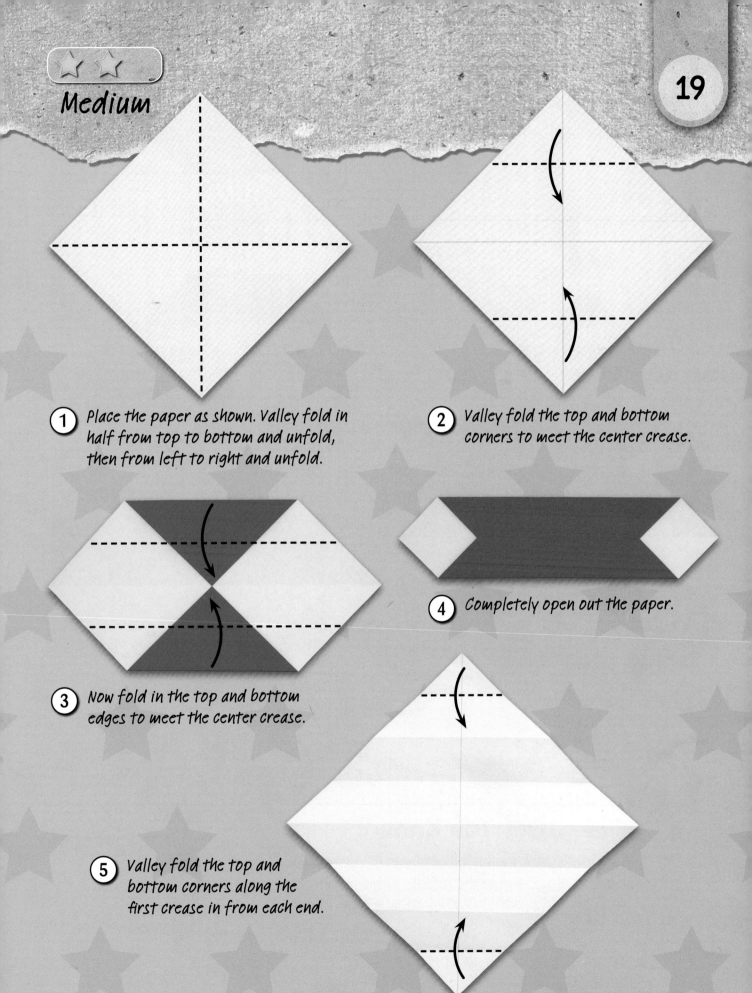

1 Place the paper as shown. Valley fold in half from top to bottom and unfold, then from left to right and unfold.

2 Valley fold the top and bottom corners to meet the center crease.

3 Now fold in the top and bottom edges to meet the center crease.

4 Completely open out the paper.

5 Valley fold the top and bottom corners along the first crease in from each end.

⑥ Fold in the top and bottom along the next crease in.

⑦ Draw the eye in the middle of the white section. Cover it up again by folding the top and bottom in once more.

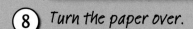

⑧ Turn the paper over.

⑨ Valley fold the left and right points to meet the center.

⑩ Make angled valley folds across the top half as shown. Crease well, then unfold.

Did You Know?

Ancient Greek myths tell of giants living in caves, each with a single eye in the middle of his forehead. They were called "cyclopes," which means "round-eyed."

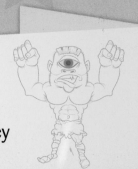

11 Make matching folds across the bottom half, and unfold.

12 Pull the top and bottom corners together on either side.

13 Pinch the points between your fingers and turn the model over.

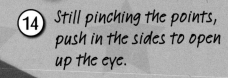

14 Still pinching the points, push in the sides to open up the eye.

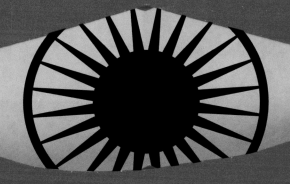

15 Once you have mastered winking, use your eerie eyeball to give your friends and family a fright!

Dracula

Watch out! This blood-sucking bad guy is searching for his next victim. Take a square of black and white paper and fold this fang-tastic vampire with some razor-sharp creases!

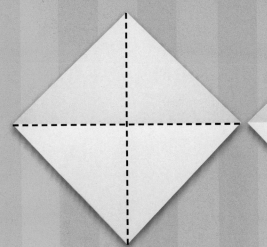

1 Place the paper as shown. Fold it in half from top to bottom and unfold, then from left to right and unfold.

2 Valley fold the top point down to meet the center.

3 Valley fold the sides as shown.

4 Turn the paper over.

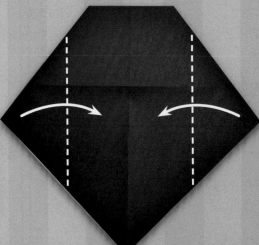

5 Valley fold the sides so that the points meet on the center crease.

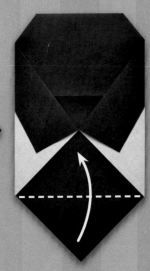

6 Fold up the bottom point.

Did You Know?

In the Middle Ages, people thought that vampires hated garlic, so they hung garlic around their necks to protect themselves!

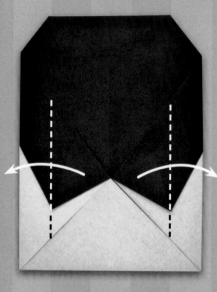

OPEN

⑦ Valley fold the side flaps about ¹/2 inch (15 mm) from either edge.

⑧ Your paper should look like this. Undo the folds you just made.

⑨ Open up the right flap.

⑩ Take the bottom point on the flap and pull it to the right. Flatten the paper.

⑪ Repeat steps 9 and 10 on the left flap. These points make Dracula's cape collar.

12 Valley fold the bottom corners.

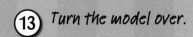

13 Turn the model over.

14 Give your Dracula eyes, eyebrows and a pointy nose. Now add a gaping mouth with frightful fangs!

Loch Ness Monster

Hard

This mysterious Scottish monster is said to live in the deep, dark waters of Loch Ness. This model shows "Nessie" lifting her head above the water, before she sinks back down below!

① Start with the paper colored side down and one point towards you. Fold it in half from left to right, then unfold.

② Valley fold the sides from the top corner so that the edges meet in the center. This makes a kite shape.

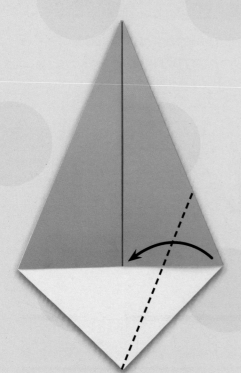

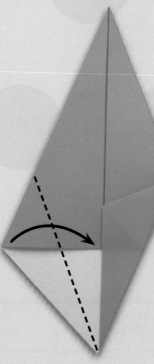

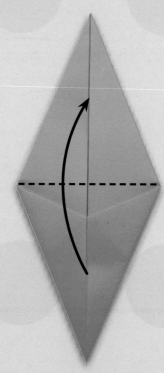

③ Fold in the right point to meet the center crease.

④ Do the same with the left point.

⑤ Valley fold the paper from bottom to top.

Did You Know?

Since 1933, people have reported seeing humps, bumps, and serpent-like shapes in Loch Ness, making Nessie world-famous!

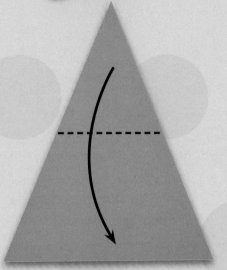

6 Valley fold the upper layer so that the top point meets the bottom edge.

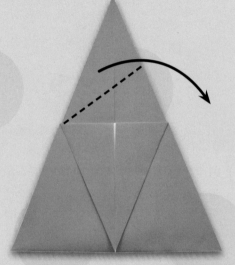

7 Fold the top point on the lower layer over to the right to make a stretched triangle.

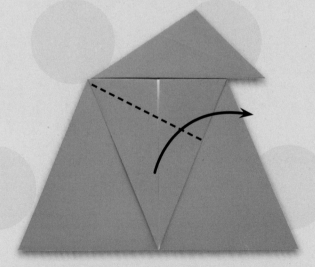

8 Fold the bottom point over in the same way.

9 Valley fold the top triangle using the crease you made earlier as a guide.

10 Open out the fold you just made.

11 Now completely unfold the point.

12 Make an inside reverse fold, tucking the right edge inside.

13 Fold the paper back down to the stretched triangle shape.

14 Now valley fold the lower triangle using the crease you made earlier as a guide.

15 Open out the fold you just made.

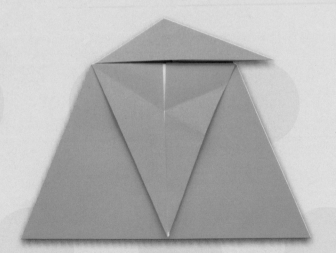

16 Now completely unfold the point.

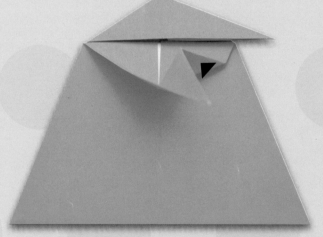

17 Tuck the right edge in with an inside reverse fold. Then fold the paper back down to the stretched triangle shape.

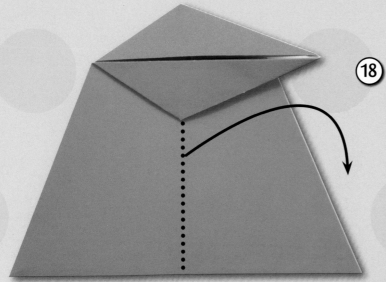

18 The monster's head is complete. Now mountain fold the right side behind the left side to shape the long, thin neck.

19 Draw an eye on the top of the head. Your mystery monster of the deep is ready to make a rare appearance!

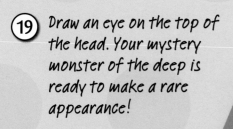

Glossary

crease A line in a piece of paper made by folding.

eerie Strange and frightening.

loch The word used for "lake" in Scotland.

menace A person or thing that is likely to be harmful or dangerous.

Middle Ages The period in European history from the 5th to the 15th century.

mountain fold An origami step where a piece of paper is folded so that the crease is pointing upwards, like a mountain.

mysterious Something that is difficult or impossible to understand.

myths Ancient stories that are often about strange events that cannot easily be explained.

phantom A ghost.

prowl Move quietly, trying not to be seen or heard.

serpent A large snake.

step fold A mountain fold and valley fold next to each other.

valley fold An origami step where a piece of paper is folded so that the crease is pointing downwards, like a valley.

Further Reading

Akass, Susan. *My First Origami Book*. Cico Kidz, 2011.
Biddle, Steve & Megumi Biddle. *Paper Capers*. Dover Publications, 2014.
Ono, Mari & Hiroaki Takai. *Dinogami*. Cico Books, 2012.
Robinson, Nick & Susan Behar. *Origami XOXO*. Ivy Press, 2012.

Index